CW00394941

LO

Inspiration and Guidance for Daily Living

A *Jesus in My Pocket* Book

That Christ may dwell in your hearts through faith; that you, being rooted and grounded in love, may be able to comprehend with all the saints what is the width and length and depth and height—to know the love of Christ which passes knowledge; that you may be filled with all the fullness of God.

Ephesians 3:17-19

Thomas Nelson Publishers
Nashville

Walking in Love with Jesus
Inspiration and Guidance for Daily Living
A *Jesus in My Pocket* Book
Copyright © 1999
Jesus in My Pocket, Inc.

Jesus in My Pocket Ministries
PMB #327
6632 Telegraph Road
Bloomfield, MI 48301

All Scripture quotations are taken from the
New King James Version of the Bible
Copyright © 1982
Thomas Nelson, Inc.
Used by permission.

All Rights Reserved
Printed in Mexico
1 2 3 4 5 6 . . . 04 03 02 01 00 99

When I walk in love with Jesus...

I remember that God always holds the key to any dilemma. As long as I keep Jesus by my side, and love in my heart, I will be guided and counseled.

God's Word says...

Ask, and it will be given to you; seek, and you will find; knock, and it will be opened to you. For everyone who asks receives, and he who seeks finds, and to him who knocks it will be opened.

Matthew 7:7-8

Just for You

Jesus in My Pocket

Fold Here

FROM: ____________________

TO: ____________________

____

When I walk in love with Jesus...

I honor all my relationships, no matter how fleeting. Behind every face is the image of God. Knowing that, and keeping it in my heart, helps me express love to others even when they are angry or unkind towards me.

God's Word says...

The stranger who dwells among you shall be to you as one born among you, and you shall love him as yourself; for you were strangers in the land of Egypt: I am the LORD your God.

Leviticus 19:34

Just for You

Jesus in My Pocket

Fold Here

FROM: ____________________

TO: ____________________

____

When I walk in love with Jesus...

I learn to love my children unconditionally. Even when I feel they haven't lived up to my expectations, I will love them for the individuals that they are, and I will remember they are God's gift to me.

God's Word says...

And be kind to one another, tenderhearted, forgiving one another, even as God in Christ forgave you.

Ephesians 4:32

Just for You

Jesus in My Pocket

Fold Here

FROM: ____________________

TO: ____________________

____

When I walk in love with Jesus...

I live my life without regrets. I embrace the lessons I've learned and the ways I've grown through all of my experiences, no matter how painful they seem at the time. I remember to love myself, just as Jesus loves me.

God's Word says...

In this the love of God was manifested toward us, that God has sent His only begotten Son into the world, that we might live through Him.

1 John 4:9

Just for You

Jesus in My Pocket

Fold Here

FROM: ____________

TO: ____________

____

When I walk in love with Jesus...

I see beauty in all creation. I remember that people and all of nature are a direct expression of God's love and creativity, surpassed by none.

God's Word says...

O LORD, how manifold are Your works!

In wisdom You have made them all.

The earth is full of Your possessions.

Psalm 104:24

Jesus in My Pocket

Just for You

Fold Here

FROM: ____________

TO: ____________

____

When I walk in love with Jesus...

I feel blessed for having been born. Not only has the Lord given me life, He has placed within me a loving heart. I will thank Him today for this life and this heart.

God's Word says...

And the LORD God formed man of the dust of the ground, and breathed into his nostrils the breath of life; and man became a living being.

Genesis 2:7

Just for You

Jesus in My Pocket

Fold Here

FROM: ____________________

TO: ____________________

____

When I walk in love with Jesus...

I know I am never alone. Even when I do not feel loved by others, I will remember that Jesus loves me, He is always with me, and He has promised me eternal life.

God's Word says...

And the LORD, He is the One who goes before you. He will be with you, He will not leave you nor forsake you; do not fear nor be dismayed.

Deuteronomy 31:8

Just for You

Jesus in My Pocket

Fold Here

FROM: ____________________

TO: ____________________

____

When I walk in love with Jesus...

I teach my children to love the Lord. Just as I have taught them to speak, to walk, and to dress themselves, I will teach them the most important lesson of all—to honor Jesus and keep Him alive in their hearts.

God's Word says...

Train up a child in the way he should go,
And when he is old he will not depart
from it.

Proverbs 22:6

Jesus in My Pocket

Just for You

Fold Here

FROM: ____________________

TO: ____________________

____

When I walk in love with Jesus...

I am forgiving and loving to my family and my friends. I overlook their shortcomings, refrain from giving them my advice and opinions unless they're asked for, and focus on their good points.

God's Word says...

And whenever you stand praying, if you have anything against anyone, forgive him, that your Father in heaven may also forgive you your trespasses.

Mark 11:25

Just for You

Jesus in My Pocket

Fold Here

FROM: ____________________

TO: ____________________

____

When I walk in love with Jesus...

I am able to think loving thoughts about my enemies. I know it is easier to love those who love me in return, but it is a calling and commandment from the Lord to extend my love to those who are unloving towards me.

God's Word says...

But I say to you, love your enemies, bless those who curse you, do good to those who hate you, and pray for those who spitefully use you and persecute you.

Matthew 5:44

Just for You

Jesus in My Pocket

Fold Here

FROM: ____________________

TO: ____________________

____

When I walk in love with Jesus...

I do not throw love away. Instead, I try to work out differences, be honest in my communication, and appreciate the other point of view instead of walking away in anger or removing myself from the situation.

God's Word says...

The fruit of the Spirit is love, joy, peace, longsuffering, kindness, goodness, faithfulness, gentleness, self-control.

Galatians 5:22-23

Jesus in My Pocket

Just for You

Fold Here

FROM: ______________

TO: ______________

____

When I walk in love with Jesus...

I treat my children tenderly. Knowing that words can sting, I will think before speaking, offer praise instead of criticism, and always encourage them to act lovingly towards others, too.

God's Word says...

Let no corrupt word proceed out of your mouth, but what is good for necessary edification, that it may impart grace to the hearers.

Ephesians 4:29

Just for You

Jesus in My Pocket

Fold Here

FROM: ____________

TO: ____________

____

When I walk in love with Jesus...

I treat my neighbors kindly, even if they are inconsiderate of me. I know the only behavior I can control is my own, and I act lovingly towards others at all times.

God's Word says...

A new commandment I give to you, that you love one another; as I have loved you, that you also love one another.

John 13:34

Jesus in My Pocket

Just for You

Fold Here

FROM: ____________________

TO: ____________________

____

When I walk in love with Jesus...

I remember the poor. Even if I am not able to help them financially, I can offer my time, my kind words, or my loving prayers as gifts from my heart.

God's Word says...

As each one has received a gift, minister it to one another, as good stewards of the manifold grace of God.

1 Peter 4:10

Jesus in My Pocket

Just for You

Fold Here

FROM: ____________________

TO: ____________________

____

When I walk in love with Jesus...

I have no room inside me for fear. Since I know all actions are based on love or fear, I make a conscious choice to act out of love at all times, and to keep love utmost in my heart.

God's Word says...

There is no fear in love; but perfect love casts out fear, because fear involves torment. But he who fears has not been made perfect in love.

1 John 4:18

Just for You

Jesus in My Pocket

Fold Here

FROM: ____________________

TO: ____________________

____

When I walk in love with Jesus...

I cannot harbor a grudge. If I am completely filled with love, there will be no space for negative thoughts or deeds towards myself or others.

God's Word says...

If someone says, "I love God," and hates his brother, he is a liar; for he who does not love his brother whom he has seen, how can he love God whom he has not seen? And this commandment we have from Him: that he who loves God must love his brother also.

1 John 4:20-21

Just for You

Jesus in My Pocket

Fold Here

FROM: ____________

TO: ____________

____

When I walk in love with Jesus...

I am filled with compassion. As I focus on giving rather than receiving, I am able to act lovingly at all times and with true understanding. I know that compassion is another word for love.

God's Word says...

Rejoice with those who rejoice, and weep with those who weep.

Romans 12:15

Just for You

Jesus in My Pocket

Fold Here

FROM: ________________

TO: ________________

____

When I walk in love with Jesus...

I surrender to His divine plan. I stop trying to control every detail of my life and the people in it. I approach each day with the love of Christ in my heart and yield myself to His direction.

God's Word says...

But as it is written:
"Eye has not seen, nor ear heard,
Nor have entered into the heart of man
The things which God has prepared
for those who love Him."

1 Corinthians 2:9

Just for You

Jesus in My Pocket

Fold Here

FROM: ______________________

TO: ______________________

____

When I walk in love with Jesus...

I learn to honor my parents through whom I have been given life. As God has commanded me to do, I will show reverence for them, even in areas of disagreement.

God's Word says...

Honor your father and your mother, that your days may be long upon the land which the LORD your God is giving you.

Exodus 20:12

Jesus in My Pocket

Just for You

Fold Here

FROM: ____________________

TO: ____________________

____

When I walk in love with Jesus...

I strive to be helpful to others in thought, word, and deed. I try to offer aid when possible, solace instead of advice, and assistance instead of criticism.

God's Word says...

Bear one another's burdens, and so fulfill the law of Christ.

Galatians 6:2

Just for You

Jesus in My Pocket

Fold Here

FROM: ____________________

TO: ____________________

____

When I walk in love with Jesus...

I allow myself to be happy. Happiness is my God-given choice, based on His love for me. I will welcome happiness into my heart and allow it to grow, instead of focusing on pain and negativity.

God's Word says...

Happy is he who has the God of Jacob for
his help,
Whose hope is in the LORD his God.

Psalm 146:5

Jesus in My Pocket

Just for You

Fold Here

FROM: ____________________

TO: ____________________

____

When I walk in love with Jesus...

I like myself more. Knowing I have been created in the image of God is enough of a reason to be pleased with who I am, how I act, and how I look.

God's Word says...

God created man in His own image; in the image of God He created him; male and female He created them. . . . Then God saw everything that He had made, and indeed it was very good.

Genesis 1:27, 31

Just for You

Jesus in My Pocket

Fold Here

FROM: ____________________

TO: ____________________

____

When I walk in love with Jesus...

I bless my mate and our relationship. I know it is through a relationship with another that I can best express my loving nature, so I cherish our union and keep it pure in my thoughts, words and deeds.

God's Word says...

Marriage is honorable among all, and the bed undefiled; but fornicators and adulterers God will judge. Let your conduct be without covetousness; be content with such things as you have.

Hebrews 13:4-5

Just for You

Jesus in My Pocket

Fold Here

FROM: ________________

TO: ________________

____

When I walk in love with Jesus...

I develop a passion for my work and for my life. I make my every action count, I pay attention to details, and I seek the Lord's will above all.

God's Word says...

Teach me to do Your will,

For You are my God;

Your Spirit is good.

Lead me in the land of uprightness.

Psalm 143:10

Just for You

Jesus in My Pocket

Fold Here

FROM: ____________________

TO: ____________________

____

When I walk in love with Jesus...

I am able to express my joy in the Lord. My laughter and smile are gifts to me from God to use and share as much as possible. I will thank God for them and treasure His blessings.

God's Word says...

Rejoice in the Lord always. Again I will say, rejoice! Let your gentleness be known to all men.

Philippians 4:4-5

Jesus in My Pocket

Just for You

Fold Here

FROM: ________________

TO: ________________

____

When I walk in love with Jesus...

I delight in His name and I keep it on my lips at all times. I remember to thank Jesus for all my pleasures and not just call on Him when I'm in trouble. I worship Him above all.

God's Word says...

Therefore by Him let us continually offer the sacrifice of praise to God, that is, the fruit of our lips, giving thanks to His name.

Hebrews 13:15

Just for You

Jesus in My Pocket

Fold Here

FROM: ____________________

TO: ____________________

____

When I walk in love with Jesus...

I pray with all my heart and soul. My prayers are filled with gratitude for my blessings, especially for the love I receive every minute of every day from Jesus Christ my Lord.

God's Word says...

Continue earnestly in prayer, being vigilant in it with thanksgiving.

Colossians 4:2

Jesus in My Pocket

Just for You

Fold Here

FROM: ____________________

TO: ____________________

____

When I walk in love with Jesus...

I keep my words soft and kind and do not wound others with my tongue. I will remember that all people are God's creation, and I will keep love in my heart for them.

God's Word says...

Let your speech always be with grace, seasoned with salt, that you may know how you ought to answer each one.

Colossians 4:6

Jesus in My Pocket

Just for You

Fold Here

FROM: ____________________

TO: ____________________

____

When I walk in love with Jesus...

I do not fear death. Just as I know I am not flesh and bones but soul and spirit, I know I will have eternal life as Jesus has promised me.

God's Word says...

But now Christ is risen from the dead, and has become the firstfruits of those who have fallen asleep. For since by man came death, by Man also came the resurrection of the dead. For as in Adam all die, even so in Christ all shall be made alive.

1 Corinthians 15:20-22

Just for You

Jesus in My Pocket

Fold Here

FROM: ____________________

TO: ____________________

____

When I walk in love with Jesus...

I learn to resist temptation. I keep my body as the holy temple God intended it to be. I resist the urge to speak unkindly or act impurely. I call on the power of God's love to overcome greed, anger, and lust.

God's Word says...

Let no one say when he is tempted, "I am tempted by God"; for God cannot be tempted by evil, nor does He Himself tempt anyone. But each one is tempted when he is drawn away by his own desires and enticed.

James 1:13-14

Just for You

Jesus in My Pocket

Fold Here

FROM: ______________

TO: ______________

____

When I walk in love with Jesus...

I keep one day set apart as holy for Him. I will bless the work He has given me on every other day, but on the Sabbath I will rest in His love.

God's Word says...

Remember the Sabbath day, to keep it holy. Six days you shall labor and do all your work, but the seventh day is the Sabbath of the LORD your God.

Exodus 20:8-10

To accept Jesus Christ as your personal Lord and Savior, pray out loud:

Heavenly Father,
I come to You in the name of Jesus. I believe in my heart that Jesus Christ is the Son of God, that He died on the Cross for my sins and was raised from the dead for my justification. I believe in my heart, and I now confess with my mouth that Jesus is Lord. Therefore, I am saved!